MANSUN

Tax-loss Lovers from Chester

Mick Middles

First published in Great Britain in1998 by Chameleon Books
an imprint of André Deutsch Ltd
76 Dean Street
London W1V 5HA

André Deutsch Ltd is a subsidiary of VCI plc
www.vci.co.uk

Design: Neal Townsend for JMP Ltd
Picture research: Karen Tucker for JMP Ltd

The right of Mick Middles to be identified as the author of this work has been asserted by him in
accordance with the Copyright, Designs and Patents act 1988

This is an unofficial book and is in no way connected with Mansun or their management,
publishing or record companies.

1 3 5 7 9 10 8 6 4 2

Printed and bound by Butler and Tanner, Frome and London

A catalogue record for this book is available from the British Library

ISBN 0 233 99350 9

MANSUN

Tax-loss Lovers from Chester

AVENUE OF INFLUENCE

[December 1976. (Punk year zero). At a party in a terraced house, Slade Lane, Levenshulme, Manchester.]

Sitting on the edge of the sofa, drawing thoughtfully on an Embassy and casting camp eyes to the ceiling, the man who was famously leaving Manchester's premier punk band, The Buzzcocks, was holding court. He cast Beefheartian expressions across the room.

'I LIKE ICE CREAM. NEW!!!'

The fanzine writer with the tape recorder flinched. It was difficult to comprehend this train of thought, let alone think of a suitable follow up question.

'Are you glam, Howard. Are you glam rock?'

Howard Devoto laboriously dragged his gaze down to the floor.

'To be glam, to be intelligently glam, that's the thing. That's the way. Achieve that, and you have achieved the surreal. You have discovered the romance. Not many people can do that. No punk bands. None. That's why I have floated away. There must be something else.'

A foglike silence crowded the room. Howard Devoto, ex-Buzzcock, future leader of Magazine; a surreal, intelligent and truly glam-art rock band of the late seventies, waved his interrogator aside and began giggling in the ear of his girlfriend, Linder. Paul Morley stood up and placed a Stooges record on the stereo then danced absurdly across the room. The New York Dolls fanatic, Steven Morrissey, slipped shyly from the scene. Intelligently glam. The phrase would strongly flavour his work a decade later.

Howard Devoto had flirted with fame, wearied of it and eventually retired to work in a photo lab in

North London. He would be awakened from his happy slumber in 1997 by a new band. An intelligently glam band. A surreal, romantic, mad lad, bad band from the world's most unlikely rock'n'roll town, Chester.

Somehow, Devoto's message had filtered down the years. Magazine, had been brilliant, maddening, invigorating and depressing. A mass of paradoxes. Too clever by half, to take the big prize. But this new band from Chester, named Mansun, seemed strangely able to take the intelligence and the sense of paradox, onto a

larger stage. A much larger stage. Even America.

Glam, if stretched too far, or fired by too much thought can fall into the realms of perversity. And Mansun are nothing if not perverse. Having just blasted straight through America, and with their biggest US hit Wide Open Space beginning to fill slots normally reserved for U2 and REM, one might have expected them to return to Britain in a triumphant flurry. Not so. The one mighty song that graced their October 1997 EP, the sure-fire

mega-hit, The World's Still Open, had been sneaked into the shadows at the rear of the CD. Deliberately shielded, it was hiding behind three wildly esoteric stabs at shunting their sound around. The coup though, was the voice on the previous track, Everyone Must Win. The voice of Howard Devoto. Still absurd after all these years.

October 1997
Tunbridge Wells Forum

A strange place to warm up for a short, sharp British tour. A dull hell hole on top of a hill, stuffed with journos and bods from the music biz. A secret gig, of sorts, for inevitably word had seeped out. Further proof that everything about this band is odd. Even in the refined atmosphere of 'those who were in the know' Mansun proved difficult to pin down. Many people would have been seduced by the soft production sheen that thickly coated their wildly eccentric number one debut album, Attack Of The Grey Lantern. Add to this the notion of a band fresh from teasing the US stadium circuit and one might have been expecting to see something rather controlled.

Not so. The startled Tunbridge audience were treated to a breathless, spikily ragged set, where even the vastness of the hit, Wide Open Space, was trimmed down and smashed across in almost punk fashion. The same too, of their clever-clever smart-arse of a song, Taxloss. Performed on this stage, it lost all of its entrancing subtlety – rather like The Ramones attacking Pink Floyd. Just to pummel everyone well and truly into confusion, their new, hopelessly inaccessible lead song from the CD, Closed For Business, was completely stripped of its esoteric harpsichord weirdness, and was thrashed across with unexpected aplomb. This night was turning into 1977.

It was a strange sight. Who did this band think they were, playing so flippantly with our rock

history? Could we trust them? As more than one critic pointed out, Mansun are a fake. A damn good fake but a fake nonetheless.

But are they? This is a parochial band. For months, visually and musically, they have careered through the genres and fads of the past twenty years of rock without a care in the world. Often taking great delight in parading themselves in the slightly naff and the ungainly – in fashions that appeared very late in the life of particular fads. Reni hats, safety pins, houndstooth suits, floppy bleached Britpop mop tops. Maybe Mansun are the ultimate revenge of provincial rock. A monster created out there returning to haunt us.

It is no accident that Chester should produce a band powered by such diverse influences, for it is a strange city, full of paradox and extremes. Every day tourists pump into the city centre; glassy eyed Americans merging with packs of French schoolchildren. Beige-clad pensioners and moony newlyweds mix with bearded bike gangs and deranged sub-punks. It is a Roman city bristling with modern designer outlets. By day a safe tourist spot but as night bites it can be as riotous as any town in Britain. The pubs are full of post-match soccer hooligans and the gutters bulge with the debris of those who have taken it a little too far.

Geographically, it is at the centre of Britain. Liverpool sprawls to the north, Manchester to the east and North Wales, with its own peculiar brand of punky street youth, is just a skip away to the west. It sits beside an area of great wealth – the Cheshire Plain – and Wrexham. It is a strip of borderlands where genuine Welsh patriotism rubs eternally against the might of England. Welsh pride against English apathy. The heavy industry of Deeside with its dour, edgy estates, lies next to lush farmlands.

The city layout is also curious. Within the

'To be glam, to be intelligently glam, that's the thing. That's the way. Achieve that, and you have achieved the surreal.'

Howard Devoto

Roman walls it is as numbingly beautiful as any town in England, full of medieval walkways and dark mysterious alleys and, latterly, modernistic town planning. But it never quite loses its 'edgy' feel. Perhaps it's the unhappy way the traffic is eternally gridlocked on the one way system or just the way the cider-swilling punks leer at gawping tourists. Maybe it's the uneasy mix of Manc and Scouse, for the accents clash at every crossroads. Whatever it is, walking around Chester is slightly unnerving, the veneer of respectability seeming precariously thin.

Chester is embedded deep within the music of Mansun – and vice versa. The music suits the town and it's not difficult to imagine it swirling down the high streets, soundtracking the daily chaos. Many of the bizarre characters who live in Paul Draper's lyrics could have been plucked directly from the precinct around the Cathedral. How many of the early songs were composed while Draper drifted through the town, soaking in the underlying weirdness? Almost all of them, I'd suggest, as Draper – and Stove and Chad come to that – remain ferociously attached to the city. The scene from which

Mansun emerged was tight-knit, proud and not at all used to producing major pop stars so the affection is a two-way affair. As the songs pour from the prolific Paul Draper – 36 written and released in eighteen months – and the band rise into the world's spotlight, this affection for Chester appears to strengthen.

The revenge of provincial rock seems all the more obvious as you wander through Chester. All manner of fad, garment and genre can be found there, crouching in defunct shop doorways, huddling in green-haired bonhomie, wandering lonely as a goth into the Virgin Megastore. Parkas mingle with baggy, floppy, tight and glam. All are there. Their allegiances made slightly perverse by lapses of time and geography. Very Mansun. Proud, detached, weird and ultimately rather interesting.

9

CHAPTER ONE

If Mansun's swift musical evolvement owes much to this sense of detachment, their visual appearance which always confounds and often amuses, also seems to be a warped reflection of the fashions on those streets. In the eighteen months it took them to rise to their unlikely prominence, their image encapsulated everything – and often at the same time.

'A long, warped fashion show,' as the NME neatly put it... 'from post baggy gonks in casual threads to polysexual mods in make up, frilly shirts and safety pins...almost as if they were dressed by colour-blind art terrorists from the Playschool costume department.'

Mansun have always managed to exact gasps of disbelief from supposedly sophisticated onlookers in Britain and abroad. But there is something comic and courageous, something rather profound even, in the way they mix and match classic pop uniforms. Yet somehow they manage to get away with it. How have they managed this?

Singer/songwriter Paul Draper has always strived to play down this sense of sartorial cleverness, choosing to tell the NME, in 1997, 'At the start we didn't have a fucking clue what we were doing. We just wore anything. We've fucked up a few times and have probably grown up in public, but now I think it's important to do whatever you want...like the Manic Street Preachers. They wanna be big as well. They come from a small town. But the reality is that we are just four lads from Chester. I've got Doc Martins and I've got Adidas trainers and I wear both.'

Paul Draper isn't originally from Chester. He was born in Wavertree, Liverpool, to a Catholic mother and Protestant father. He was sent to a Catholic school where, he claims, the nuns used to hit the pupils while instilling their indelible strain of guilt. Draper's father worked on the Liverpool docks, his background firmly entrenched in the dizzying polemics of a rapidly shrinking industry. The 1960s and '70s saw Liverpool's shipbuilding decimated and this, Britain's most dramatic industrial collapse of the twentieth century, sank deep into the Liverpudlian psyche. The city's heart frequently only finding voice in its proud affiliations with football and music.

But work was near impossible to find and consequently, when Paul was eleven, the Draper family moved to the industrial flatlands of Deeside, on the fringe of North Wales. His father picked up bits of work, here and there, as a hod-carrier and building-site labourer.

It was in Deeside, twelve months later, that Paul decided to take up the guitar. It was not a practice that particularly endeared him to his peers and he was regularly picked on and bullied for stubbornly persevering with his instrument. Draper's anger at a seemingly Philistine world can be traced back to the day when, walking home from school, his treasured guitar under his arm, he was viciously set upon by locals. Sinking to a level of stupidity that still astonishes him today, they beat him black and blue while smashing his guitar against the wall, leaving a tangle of wood, strings and a sobbing boy with a newly formed grudge against the world.

The prevailing football town mentality would brand him a further outcast. Always a staunch Evertonian, he was unable to join in the local banter and was mercilessly derided and continually attacked especially as, in his own admission, he always looked strikingly feminine. As the years passed Draper would learn to channel his anger into creative energy. 'I learned to sit back and observe,' he would

later state. Undoubtedly, his seething anger has heavily flavoured his songwriting. Slowly, many of his schoolyard peers started to respect him, not least for his increasingly extensive record collection and subsequent musical knowledge that extended far beyond the average. 'The kids from school...even some of the ones who used to be really nasty, started coming round to our house, simply to listen to the music and hear me enthusing about it. It was often at lunch time and, in a funny kind of way, those records provided me with an identity. I wasn't just some dumb kid who didn't like football anymore...although I do like football, I see the magic in it, but it's just not the centre of my entire existence.'

The disparate nature of his swelling record collection became strongly reflected in his choice of clothing. He wore mainly cheap, rock-tinged fashions, culled from the dingy cult shops of Chester, Wrexham and Rhyl. Musically,

Paul Draper ripped through the genres, from punk to hip hop, always sensing nothing wrong with liking U2 at the same time as nurturing an understanding of NWA and Public Enemy. He simply soaked in anything he deemed good, original or just plain absurd.

Quite in which category one might place Doctor Who remains open to question. Since the age of four, Draper has loved our cosy sci-fi Doctor. He even admitted forming a huge crush on Lalla Ward, Doctor Who's assistant Romana who, in real life, married Tom Baker.

Draper would also make irregular forays across Snowdonia to the Gwynedd Italianate village of Porthmerion, the location for his all time favourite TV show, The Prisoner. He would later tell the NME that, 'I spent countless summers running up and down the beach shouting, "I am a free man" and wearing black suits...' Presumably his tongue was firmly lodged in his cheek. Nevertheless, considerable

hours and days were spent mooning about Clough Williams Ellis' wildly eccentric village creation. Draper saw the village as a blast of refreshing absurdity nestling in an area of cultural conservatism. Much, perhaps, like his forthcoming band.

Paul's family remained staunch Liverpudlian socialists, with all his uncles being disenfranchised dockers or retired merchant seamen. As such, his upbringing placed him naturally on the left, although the absurdities of a desperate left wing attempting to retain some kind of power wouldn't be lost on him. More than that he would glean inspiration from the hopelessness of it all. As he later stated, to the NME. '...As far as I could always see, Britain lost its soul. It feels like it has no soul for a fight anymore, and probably the miner's strike crushed all that. Deep down, if there was any political philosophy I would subscribe to, it would be communism. I think any right thinking human being would be communist at heart, yet the reality is that you can't defeat human nature. And human nature is greedy, back from cavemen days when the biggest cavemen beat up the smallest cavemen and got the fittest women. That's basically the structure of things and it hasn't changed. I saw it, full on, when I was growing up. Everything was collapsing and, at the very heart of it all, was human nature, screwing things up from all angles. Impossible to beat but endlessly interesting.' Very Mansun.

Mansun as a band, began in and around the geographical – and cultural – triangle of Wrexham, Chester and Liverpool. More famously, *the moment* happened at Wrexham Art College when Paul Draper, bored to tears with his endless attempts to fit his highly individual notion of art into any kind of curriculum, met the equally bored Stove King, actually a student at Liverpool Graphic Art College. King, who hailed from Ellesmere Port, ten miles to the north of Deeside and who was rather more firmly embedded in the commuter belt of Liverpool, felt an unusual empathy with his existential new friend and a working liaison was instant. Much to their surprise, they soon found themselves working, side by side, in the same photo laboratory and, at lunchtimes, relaxed in Chester's Fat Cat pub where they met the third essential part of the triangle, guitarist and hedonist, Dominic Chad. Having abandoned his languages degree – he was expelled from his Russian and French classes at Bangor University, he drifted vaguely inland. Social forces guided him towards Chester, where he secured work as the Fat Cat bar manager.

Chad was another oddity. Born in Cheltenham, he had nurtured a life long obsession with local guitar tragi-hero, Rolling Stone, Brian Jones. At various times in his life, Chad has claimed to be in spiritual contact with Jones who has remained an omnipresent shadow within Chad's curious psyche. A muse perhaps. An inspiration, definitely.

Falling together, more as a huddle of ideas than as a band, they initially named themselves Green Lantern, after the American comic-book hero who surfaced in one of Draper's songs. It was hopefully also supposed to sound a little bit like Pink Floyd. When a rehearsal studio lackey pointedly informed them that Green Lantern was easily the worst name of any of the crap bands who had filled his practice rooms with nauseating cacophony, they decided to switch to 'A Man Called Sun', after a favourite Verve B side. Eventually, it was their publisher who decided the name was rather similar to A Man Called Adam, and it was duly truncated to Mansun.

Before procuring a drummer, Hib, and original fifth member, sampler/effects man, Mark, into their gang, Mansun set up with a drum sampler in a room at Liverpool's Crash rehearsal studios. It had previously been occupied by Terry Hall's Colourfield and various incarnations of The Lightning Seeds. Early Mansun demos would feature the band thrashing about punkily over the top of a cracking, melody crushing breakbeat. Hib, undoubtedly, was a welcome addition.

Time off from Sunday rehearsals would mean a trip to the nearby 'sad rock fart' club, The Tivoli, in Buckley, where the lads enjoyed the absurdity of sinking into alcoholic dementia to the sound of Rainbow, Led Zeppelin and Hendrix. This rock atmosphere had an interesting effect on the embryonic band, especially as they bravely blagged themselves the odd gig in the place. As such, the first three Mansun gigs were, to appease the leery, beery regulars, performed at a stupidly ear splitting level. It wasn't a hugely auspicious start, for the small Liverpool audiences believed them to be little more than a joke; a strange combination of rock and pop.

Stove: 'We are still a standing joke in Liverpool. Yeah...they thought we were the worst bullshitter, part-time knobheads going because we didn't listen to the same bands as them and we wouldn't jump on any bandwagons. When we played in front of indie fans, they all thought we weren't cool enough. But... we always loved great music, no matter where it came from and we never relied on some journalist to tell us what's hip.'

But the seeds had already been sown. Cornily, a drifting A & R man, in Liverpool to brief the rather more famous band who rehearsed across the corridor, was drawn to the spirited noise which seeped from Mansun's rehearsal rooms. He managed to prise a demo tape from the band despite their protestations: 'But it's crap...we are working on much better material now...'

The brittle half-formed songs accompanied his drive back to London and his interest caused ripples among London's close-knit A&R circle. So, without really trying and before they had captured anything more than a few dirges on tape, Mansun had already managed to create that all important A & R buzz.

Stove: 'It's true that people in London began talking about us from a very early stage and that always struck me as being a little odd because I knew lots of musicians, really great musicians too, who never, in years and years and years even managed to get their tapes listened to...it just started happening for us.'

Legend has it that Mansun were, at one stage, using the moniker *Manson*, and encouraging an affiliation with the deranged hippie murderer, but this isn't quite the case. There was a simple mix up when, the band ordered 500 T-shirts, all of which were delivered bearing the legend 'MANSON'. So, for a while, the truth was clouded by a simple spelling mistake and a batch of T-shirts that simply had to be sold. At this point, somewhat incredibly, Charles Manson's record company decided to sue this bunch of limey no hopers.

'That whole Charles Manson thing was just a complete and utter fuck up,' stated Paul Draper. 'Nothing more than a stupid fucking spelling mistake but it was just one more thing that got twisted into something perverse. It was nothing, absolutely nothing at all and then it got caught up in our madness...in our rollercoaster.'

MADNESS, MADNESS AND MORE MADNESS!

[September 1995 The A&R talk intensified and soon the Mansun phone began to ring with numbing regularity.]

Wisely however, these initial stirrings were abruptly pushed away. 'Actually we were fucking terrified,' Draper would later admit. 'I mean, we could hardly play a note and these guys were chasing us.'

The band, staying true to their punk roots, pressed up 1,000 copies of their most complete song, Take It Easy Chicken. The song, pulled straight off their best demo to date, was actually placed on both sides of the vinyl, as further recording costs were completely out of the question. The DIY process was a somewhat romantic nod back to Howard Devoto's Buzzcocks and their first, impoverished – and, as far as a Devoto-led Buzzcocks were concerned, only foray onto vinyl, Spiral Scratch, one of Paul Draper's all-time favourite EPs. There was no artwork, as such, which seems rather strange considering that this

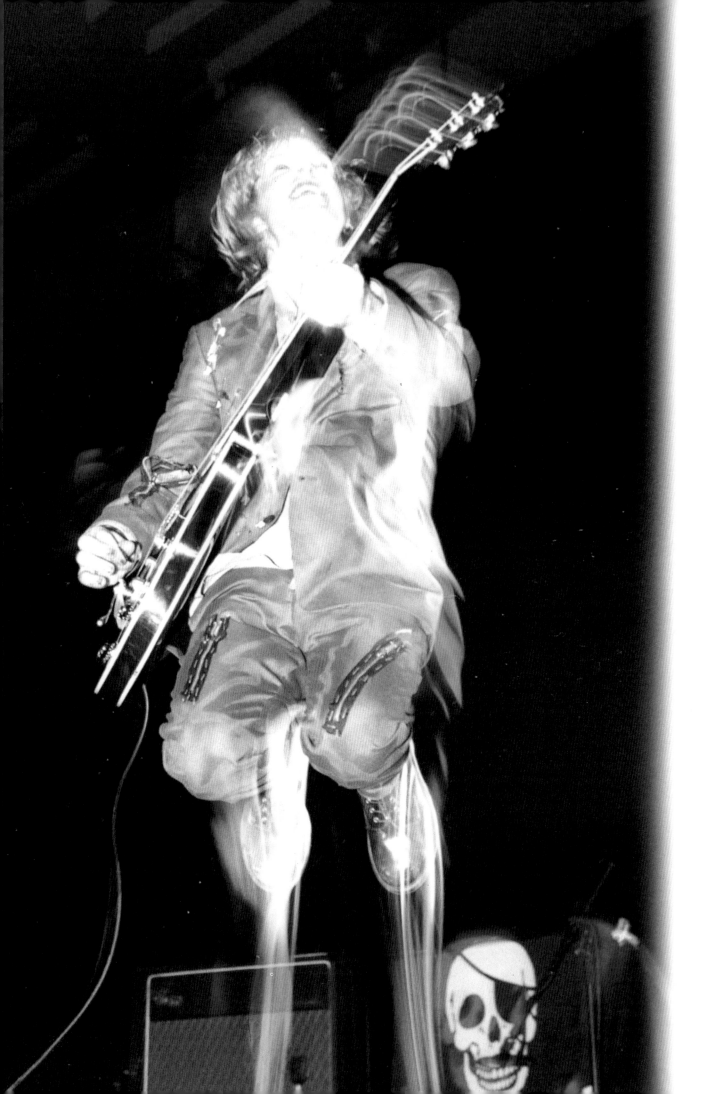

band contained two ex-graphics students. The white labels were adorned with a simplistic stamp, which scruffily screamed MANSUN!

'That first release? Madness everywhere. We didn't have a clue what was happening,' Draper has since admitted.

And it was madness, too. Take It Easy Chicken was a hook-laden song that immediately wrong-footed those expecting this bunch of lads, who looked little more than another sub-Oasis band, to actually sound like another sub-Oasis band. But Steve Lamacq, on Radio One's Evening Session , started repeatedly plugging the song and naturally it filtered onto the daytime airwaves – an astonishing achievement for a first single. Mansun's dizzying ascent had begun. John Peel, perhaps predictably, had grasped the disc with a numbing fervour too, enticing the band down to

the famous Maida Vale studios, from where their intriguing, spirited session was broadcast in November 1995.

Further support was provided by The Charlatans' Tim Burgess (The Charlatans still lived in the neighbouring town of Northwich and were acutely attuned to anything remotely interesting happening in their parish), who persuaded the stunned hopefuls to provide crazed support spots. It seemed the ascent had truly begun.

And so had the madness. From this point they hurtled full pelt into a daily cycle of extreme rock'n'roll hedonism with Chad, seemingly lost when not smashing a guitar against a wall, leaving a messy trail of destruction among many bewildered small-time hoteliers of Britain. It was a pity, in a sense, for Mansun's madness came before any form of print media (other than the

Take It Easy Chicken Drastic Sturgeon The Greatest Pain Moronica

Mansun

TWO EP

occasional and extremely tentative NME article) had started to show the remotest interest.

'Yeah...it was such a waste,' stated a later, rather more sober Chad. 'I was. . .we was, totally smashed for a full twelve months. I mean, really, really wild at times and nobody took a blind bit of notice. We made Led Zeppelin seem like Christmas-time advocaat drinkers. If we were like that now, we'd be rock'n'roll legends. Typical. We got the timing all wrong.'

Paul Draper. 'We were sucked into a whirl of alcohol, drugs and women. Our early gigs were total mayhem. We'd get completely off our faces, go out and play thinking, wow, this is fucking amazing. While the audience would have their fingers in their ears, screaming, "What the fuck was that?" Sometimes I couldn't blame them. There was a spell when we allowed our live gigs to

deliberately go off at a tangent. . .we just rolled along with the energy into. . .something else. I can't really explain it but it was a bit dangerous because there was a danger that the songwriting would get lost in the energy. That we'd just be a live band. . .a full-blooded, fucking fantastic live act. . .but you have to be more than that. And we knew we had greater depth but, as the rollercoaster went on and on, it seemed impossible to stop it. I think that's why we were so off our faces. We were in a state of panic.'

It wasn't always fantastic though. There are reports of early gigs where the thrust of instantaneous energy would dissolve into broken cacophony, stirring aggression in the audience and leaving the band lost, dazed and hopelessly inarticulate onstage. 'Yeah,' agreed Chad. 'Like a bunch of useless Sid Viciouses, floundering

C H A P T E R   T W O

'1 think drugs destroy bands, destroy personalities, destroy music. You have gotta know the time and the place to have a party!'

Paul Draper

around. . .true, it did get like that. Fuck knows how we survived.'

Although a Blank Generation punk wipe-out is not a bad place for a band to discover its foundations, there is a limit to hedonism, as Draper explained. 'We went right over that limit and I don't really say that in any kind of macho-oh-weren't-we-wild way because it was pretty stupid. To have to get paralytic just to play a gig. I can't believe we are still here. It was pure Sex Pistols. . .yeah, not always fantastic. Often crap. To be honest, I can't believe we are still here. We should have been buried at birth. At one point I did think it was the end of everything. The band was just falling apart. . .we couldn't communicate with each other. We'd have band meetings and just stare blankly. Fucking bunch of hopeless tossers, basically. And I have no time for all that business where rock bands start feeling sorry for themselves. Either do it or fuck off and get a job. I understand why fans think that sometimes and with us they would have been fucking right.

Although later it seems as though Mansun just climbed and climbed. . .during that first stupid, pissed year, which often seemed to be going on forever, I never thought we'd start. The audiences were growing, everything was growing but what a fucking mess we were.

'1 thought I was gonna die a few times. Like when we had to cancel one gig – it was the first gig at Tunbridge Wells – because I was in some hotel, just stiff. Couldn't move. Couldn't move my arms, legs or anything. Completely gone. I was like that for two days. . .and that was serious.'

Later, as if to emphasize the difference between the dazed, inebriated Mansun of the early days and the professional, not-quite-so-pissed band of 1997 hit-album status, Draper observed: 'I think drugs destroy bands, destroy personalities, destroy music. You have gotta know the time and the place to have a party!'

Oasis mania had bitten deep. Wave after wave of sub-Britpop, mop-topped, '60s-styled guitar gangs erupted into the country's smaller venues,

18

queuing up to act the role of screwed-up, foul-mouthed footy yob for the benefit of any passing hack. For A & R men, scurrying from dive to dive, attempting to focus on anything remotely original, the situation seemed particularly desperate. Throughout 1995 it had been difficult to catch the occasional photograph of Mansun and not place them in the same category, for they would scowl into as many cameras as possible, their hair flowing down over their shades. The odds against any band, however blessed with innovatory twists and hooks, rising from this mass with anything more than a passing minor hit single, must have been enormous.

But Mansun were different. You could sense it as they trudged around the country picking up devotees along the way as well as gathering more and more A & R interest.

They reached the peak of their unsigned existence with a Radio One showcase at the Camden Underworld. A small event that saw them perform in front of a friendly array of record company personnel, all encouraging each other with forecasts of the millions to be made from this strange little band from Chester. Nobody, at that gig could have any doubt that Mansun would soon be hurtling towards the charts. The only question would be whether or not they contained enough depth to be able to stretch their success beyond that huddle of initial singles, onto other continents and into other markets. Instant success was an easy prediction. Longevity was rather more difficult to achieve.

But the A & R men were beginning to get a taste of something special. As the initial scramble mutated into serious bidding, the band found themselves plagued by phone calls.
'Yeah, we had record company people coming up with all sorts of ridiculous ideas. We'd be sitting at home and then one of them would ring and say, "Oh, we are going to Europe this weekend for a laugh, do ya wanna come?" And it would be like, "No, not really"; recalls Stove.

Better still was the day when, answering the doorbell, Chad was confronted by a prostitute holding a bottle of champagne. Like any genuine would-be rock 'n' roll star, he abruptly snatched the bottle, told her to go home and slammed the door in her face.

More pressure came at the local Chester pubs, where A & R men would even try to circulate and get to know Mansun's friends – or at least those claiming to be their friends. It was a high-pressure campaign to land the catch of the year.

THE SIGNING. . . AND A BIT MORE MADNESS.

[November-December 1995

The rest of Britain, catching sight of Mansun via a peppering of modest music press articles, could only remain unimpressed.]

What could be so special about another bunch of scuzz-baggy rockers, all too often compared to The Charlatans, Verve or, most curiously of all, Oasis with hip hop. Their second release on their own Sci Fi Hi Fi Records, Skin Up Pin Up, took the admittedly Oasis-like sonic boom of its predecessor, Take It Easy Chicken and added a fevered, neurotic beatbox slap beat that immediately caused people to make comparisons with Jesus Jones. Oasis, Verve and The Charlatans. The confusion was mounting.

Before the end of the year, however, Parlophone A & R man Keith Wozencroft had managed to capture the band's signatures. Thereby completing a neat little post-Britpop cache for EMI who, despite spending a few good years in rock's obscure shadows, would soon be boasting a roster that included Blur, Radiohead, Supergrass, The Sundays. . . and Mansun.

January 1996

The signing was swift and inevitable. Penniless, Mansun succumbed to the grabbing hand of Parlophone in the UK and Epic in the USA.

Far from allowing themselves to be bullied into an extreme commitment schedule, Mansun were intelligent enough to compose and demand a slowly evolving recording process which would see them record a series of EPs, instead of the usual quick-fire string of highly promoted singles. The idea, ironic considering the meteoric nature of their rise, was to slowly ease the band into the mainstream. A deal which would allow them time and space to develop. Not for Mansun, it seemed, the fast track to Top Of The Pops. For Draper in particular, with tunes and ideas beginning to bubble ferociously inside his head, and with a burning desire to fashion a long-term band and songwriting career, the notion of chancing everything on a couple of potential hit singles seemed particularly abhorrent. Conveniently, the band booked themselves into Angelshare Studios in Deeside which, as well as being situated, just around the corner, had also been the scene of The Stone Roses' The Second Coming recordings. Much to the amazement of the studio staff, the scruffy 'local' band arrived and promptly fell into a furious stream of recordings, spinning off from the main recording, Egg Shaped Fred. The stream of EPs that would steadily force Mansun's reputation during the course of 1996 would be grounded in that very first quality studio recording.

On The Road
January / February / March 1996

With advance money in the kitty and no guiding management team in place, the Mansun rollercoaster began to rattle with dangerous intent. Two riotous mini-tours, with Audioweb and Cast – who they had met at their Liverpool rehearsal base – preceeded the release of the first Parlophone EP, which nudged to an unexpected 37 in the national charts, surprising band and record company by easily selling all 20,000 pressed copies. The dangers of such a speedy rise, however, were all too obvious.

Draper. 'The madness just intensified. . . and intensified and a lot of the people who surrounded us seemed happy to let us spiral faster and faster into oblivion. And it would have been oblivion too, for we had absolutely no idea about direction or anything. We were acting totally on instinct. To some degree this out of control feel made us work even harder. . . I was writing furiously. I think writing was the only place where I could find some normality. . . which is pretty weird considering how surreal some of the songs are. But we really had started to attract fairly sizeable audiences, which was a complete surprise. I don't know if we were ready or not. . . better, I suppose, than playing empty halls or bottom of a load of lousy bills. But that kind of success brings with it certain other pressure. . . like not actually selling that many records. . . Oh I don't know, it was all buzzing around our heads and we dealt with it in different ways. . . Chad dealt with it in a most, let's say, excitable fashion.'

Something just had to give. The signs had been in place at the band's BRATS appearance – either a triumph or a nondescript run-through,

I think writing was the only place where I could find some normality...which is pretty weird considering how surreal some of the songs are.

Paul Draper

depending on which reviewer you chose to believe – when, according to sponsors, the NME, '. . . psychosis completely swallowed the band and spat them into the gutter.'

The mixed reviews of Mansun's BRATS set, saw Radio One claiming them to be '. . . the most exciting new band in a town full of exciting new bands. . . ' while, perhaps more interestingly and certainly more worryingly, the NME's John Robinson chose to lunge in with a double- footed tackle which crashed onto Mansun's Achilles heel. The fact that the band's look and their music, might be rather too close to the outpourings of Oasis. A charge that in retrospect seems nothing short of absurd.

Robinson was adamant. 'Then came Mansun who, remember, definitely don't sound like Oasis.

Oh no. Perish the thought. Were you, however, to entertain the flimsiest and most whimsical of hypothetical notions, you could possibly, tentatively, suggest that it was Mansun's intention to form a group in many ways similar to Oasis but with the twist that the singer would wear a hat. Still, charlatans and unprincipled opportunists though they be, they and their one decent song, Take It Easy Chicken does prove one thing, that the forecasted air of psychedelic wurbling is emerging, and that, so mad are the kids for it, they would, if asked, mosh to tosh on toast.'

It was Mansun's sixteen-year-old 'samples' expert, Mark, who fell from the rollercoaster, simply disappearing at the end of the BRATS affair. 'It wasn't really Mark's fault,' Stove would

later recall. 'I mean it had been an unbelievable ride. We'd done like thirty gigs, and we were playing in front of 2,000 people who were totally into us, being hailed as one of the best new bands in the country and it was a total head fuck.'

When the band finally managed to track him down, their hopes of guiding him back into the Mansun camp swiftly faded. 'He was in a real state, to be honest,' admitted Stove. 'Paranoid, shaking, he could hardly speak. We felt really sorry for him. I mean, at sixteen you just want to go and kick a ball with your mates, don't you? You don't want to be stuck in a studio for five weeks. It's made us all insane but, for the rest of us, it's been a positive insanity.'

We were playing in front of 2,000 people who were totally into us, being hailed as one of the best new bands in the country and it was a total head fuck.

Stove

Success, even torrid, underground live success, and a mass of record-company encouragement, can be a powerful and unruly force. Reality is held firmly in check. The problem with the violent onrush of fame is the initial realization that, however much you may gain, aspects of your former life are bound to be lost. In Stove's statement about a kid wanting to go and kick balls, might it be possible to hear the faintest hint that part of him, too, might occasionally long to return to a simpler life. But whereas at twenty Stove had just gained the maturity to understand such feelings, nobody can expect a sixteen-year-old to suddenly eclipse boyhood.

(How mature the guitarist was after the BRATS should be noted. He was so plastered after the performance that he couldn't, for the life of him,

remember in which hotel he was staying. He slumped into a cab and instructed the driver to take him to EMI headquarters. Unfortunately the cabby wasn't in tune with up-to-the-minute music biz news and duly dumped the hapless guitarist in Manchester Square, at the premises vacated by EMI several months previously. All that was left for Chad to do, therefore, was to curl up in the old EMI doorway where a kindly grey-haired security guard reached down, tapped him on the shoulder and gently told him to 'Piss off out of here.')

Mansun's fevered live activity during the spring of 1996, supporting, Audioweb, Cast and then Shed Seven continued into the summer. In its wake was left a trail of smashed hotels, Transit vans and, on occasion motorway service stations.

MANSION

At sixteen you
just want to go
and kick a ball
with your
mates, don't
you? You don't
want to be stuck
in a studio for
five weeks.

We have gone from n to equilibrium in the s

The vandalized mess was softened only by the fact that Mansun were – even to startled hoteliers – hooligans of a curiously likeable, intelligent variety. Nevertheless these were dark days. One evening Stove took offence during a spate of homophobic audience chants during a Cast support spot – a small section of the crowd stupidly honing in on the band's rather startling use of makeup – and leapt into the audience, swinging his Fender bass at the head of the main culprit. He connected. While this little fracas was spilling into a serious affray, Draper underwent a sudden attack of the Pete Townshends and smashed his guitar into the midriff of his amp stack, causing the instrument to splinter amid a frenzy of sparks. Things were beginning to get seriously out of hand.

Two days later, while on their way to Kentish Town Forum, the band were stopped on London's Westway by Anti-Terrorist Police, following a spate of IRA activity in the capital. The band were spread-eagled against a wall as machine guns hovered inches from their heads. Unfortunately, as their tour van contained a small amount of soft drugs, the police decided to transform the search into a full scale drug bust, drafting in sniffer dogs and drugs officers, who seemed to take an unhealthy delight in strip searching band and crew. Chad later admitted that the bulk of his 'stash' had been left in his hotel room.

It was par for the course, really. In Norwich the whole band were ejected from their hotel at midnight following complaints from the other guests and, in Newcastle, after evacuating the Marriott Hotel, Paul Draper and Peter from Cast ended up in police custody. Strangely, such events would lead to an eventual steadying of the band as Cast's management team of Dave Nicholl and Rob Swerdlow decided to take the band under their wing.

September 1996

Twelve months on, rumours were circulating that the band's legendary hedonism had slowed to a dull burn, a memory even, to some extent. Wheeled out and used to spit fire into the live set. Offstage, in the dressing rooms, in pubs even, their madness, their legendary imbibing would now fuel the band chatter. 'Remember when Chad. . . Oh yeah but what about that time in Luton. . .' etc.

The living, walking, talking symbol of Mansun's slowing down would be the taming of Chad. A self-styled insane guitarist pulled back from the brink. It was a close thing as a hundred gigs melted into a beery blur, and demons began to creep into Chad's every waking moment, warning him of the problems that lay ahead. It would take intelligence and strength to pull out of that particular slow dive. Without Chad's hedonism, without the sheer unbridled excess that will be forever linked with the early years of the band, surely Mansun would still be tramping the streets of Chester and Wrexham, full of dreams and indignance; full of dead hope and cynicism.

The trick though, was to keep the insanity intact onstage; to retain that full-pelt aural and visual assault; to push right to the very limit and instill, in their gawping admirers, a feeling of euphoria, untempered by the need to swap alcohol for mineral water.

And to a large extent, they succeeded. Onstage at Tunbridge Wells in September, for instance, a caricature 'out of their heads' vision flowed from all members of the band. Watching the gig, nobody, one senses, would have been surprised to see these four lads returning to their hotel and, unable to wind down, begin hurtling TVs around their rooms. Nothing unusual in that! But backstage at Tunbridge Wells, a comparative sobriety floated in the air. Beers were cracked open, for sure, but one can extract a certain irony from Chad's impassioned groan, 'For Christ's sake, where's my fucking mineral water!'

Back at the untrashed hotel room, the evening's gig was generally regarded as average by the band. Paul Draper, clutching only his second beer of the evening, explained the extent of the band's admirable alcoholic pullback.

'We used to get paralytic just to play a gig,' he told the NME's Mark Beaumont. 'It was all just a blur really. I can't believe we are still here. We should have been buried at birth. It was pure Sex Pistols. (It wasn't, actually, as The Sex Pistols couldn't out-drink a granny with a Mackeson, but that's another story.) The band was just falling apart. I thought it was the end or, more like, it'd never start. It was like, this is not meant to be. I thought I'd die a few times. Like when we had to cancel playing here last time around. I was in some hotel down the road, just stiff, couldn't move. I was like it for about two days.'

The final straw for the band's nucleus, Paul, Chad and Stove, must have been the night when an inebriated Chad, treading unsteadily into another dimension, sliced his hand open on his guitar. The sight of blood brought the other members firmly back down to earth.

'We thought we really had better draw the line after that,' said Draper. 'It's like defying gravity. We should've fallen long ago. It must be destiny to come through. We have gone from nothing to chaos and now to equilibrium in the space of nine months.'

It should be noted that Chad has been seen at the meetings of the Chester branch of Alcoholics Anonymous. An indication perhaps, of the seriousness of his addiction. Ⓜ

STRIPPER VICAR

[A sprightly, punchy, vivacious new single was also to coincide with this new found sobriety.]

Arguably their most vividly accessible
disk to date, Stripper Vicar recalled the cheekiest lyrical tantrums of Morrissey circa Queen Is Dead.
Particularly the savage little sentences bursting out through the medium of catchy chart-directed
pop. The single's plush production failed to cover images of a naked transvestite vicar
and various forms of debauched clergy. Was this satire or comic book imagery? Daft or profound?
Whatever, Stripper Vicar would survive as Mansun's most telling record. A pile-up of paradoxes at
once very serious and very lightweight. But why write a song about a man of the cloth indulging in

flamboyant disrobing before perishing in a bizarre stockings in the ear accident? Just a piece of tabloid daftness, surely.

Paul Draper. 'It's a little more serious than that. It depends on how you look at it. It is just another aspect of this bizarre world, a world in which anything can happen and often does. . . and when it does it can have a comical edge. This is a song with a comical edge alright but it also has a serious heart. I distrust all religion really. I reckon it comes from going to a horrible Catholic school with mad nuns who would kick the fuck out of you if you didn't do your homework. Since then I have viewed religion as a vehicle to confuse people. If you scratch away at the surface of anyone, no matter how prim and proper, you'll always find something sinister underneath. It's human nature, innit?' He continues, 'I'm disgusted with religion. The Catholic religion is the biggest company in the world. They have got loads of gold reserves and they harboured Nazi war criminals after the war. They'd have a big push with collections if the stock prices went down.'

Negative views on religion lie deep within Draper's psyche. He comes from a mixed Catholic/Protestant family in which his mother's Catholicism held the balance of power. The staples of Catholic schooling, the nuns, the sinner's box, all served as heavy influences.

'I always thought Catholic guilt was bollocks,' he told Q Magazine. 'But as you get older you start understanding it. How everything was viewed as bad or dirty. Catholicism is almost like a refinement of British society itself, where you never discuss sex. To me, being British is something that looks totally respectable on the surface, but that dark side is neatly tucked away, until you scratch the surface, which is what I try to do.'

There are no dull people in this band

Paul Draper

And our poor Stripper Vicar? A cartoon character in a Mansun song, a vehicle for Paul Draper's disgust. Is that one wonders, why the man had to die? 'It was good to see him die,' he cryptically informed the NME . 'IT'S FUNNY.'

Through a veil of dark Chester humour, the surrealism of Stripper Vicar couldn't fail to sound odd. During days when the notion of a rock genius is a man who fuses dull empty sentiments with a string of simplistic clichéd riffs, Stripper Vicar simply oozed cleverness.

As a studio band intent on catching the attention of those with an ear for the unusual, regardless of hype or hipness, Mansun were moving into an orbit of their own. A a live act, however, they remained more than happy to meld cliché with gimmickry. Anything, it seemed, for a laugh.

Draper. 'I went on as a vicar one night. . . and we were trying to get a vicar and a nun to support us on tour and get their kits off. But none of the venues would have it. We eventually found this guy from a strip-o-gram agency who was up for it and when our agent told the venues, they said, "But he's not a band" and we'd go, "no, he's a solo artist".'

Stripper Vicar can be regarded as the first Mansun song to seriously climb onto the radio playlists. Debuting at number 19 in the national charts, the song's prominence clashed neatly with appearances at the Reading Festival and the two T in the Park extravaganzas. (Radio One's Steve Lamacq boldly pronounced Mansun the 'band of the festival' following their storming of T in the Park).

The new Mansun drummer, Andy Rathbone, certainly helped transform the band, from a spectacle of rather fluid musical wanderings, to a harsher, punkier, powerful live unit, by way of his driving backbeat.

Rathbone, an Audi car salesman from the Blacon housing estate in Chester, had been the band's initial choice for the drum seat although, at the time, he decided to remain loyal to the local band who he was playing with. Also, after hearing an early Mansun demo tape, he informed the band that he had no intention of playing, 'Britpop shite.'

This time around it was Rathbone who virtually forced the band to allow him to join after hearing a demo of Wide Open Space. Incidentally, Rathbone is the only member of Mansun to actually come from the city of Chester. While the band profited greatly from his unwavering musicianship, he arrived at a time when, sensing a true direction for the first time, Mansun took a giant leap into the First Division. As 1996 waned, the band at last began to assert themselves as a unique, all-powerful live force. For Andy, his initiation would settle into a six-month alcoholic blur, cornily dashing from hotel to gig to studio and back again – countries flying before his eyes. The madness. . . the madness. Those months would later seem like two weeks.

Perhaps he should have heeded the initial warnings. On his very first engagement with the band he had travelled alone down to Bristol, nervous as hell, knowing that his future could very well depend on how he controlled himself during the performance. Arriving at Temple Meads station, he purchased that week's copy of the NME and confidently perused the gig guide. To his horror he discovered that the gig was, in fact, in Brighton. . . not Bristol!

A day later, he suffered a baptism of fire when he made his first appearance on the Mansun drum stool on TFI Friday, with nine million viewers looking on. 'We knew he was the right one, after all that,' remarked Paul

> **There was a guy who said that if we played Reading he would kill us. Brilliant! If someone bothered to hate us that much we must have something**

Paul Draper

Draper. 'Anyone who makes such a stupid mistake as to turn up at the wrong town, and then perform brilliantly in a situation like TFI Friday, has got to be a Mansun kind of person. There are no dull people in this band.'

Although Mansun may have tempered their own excesses during the course of 1996, they were forced to concede that in many respects they had failed to deliver their dubious new stance to their fans. Not their fault, of course. It wouldn't sell anyway. But the hell-bent, take-it, do-it, drink-it, fuck-it image would linger a while and certainly wouldn't be altered by the sight of Chad's bottle of Evian water sitting by the bass amp.

Out there, in that scary place the audience, the 24-hour party was still raging. The summer 1996 tour was spiced by crazed incident. Nutters appeared to be attracted to Mansun. On one occasion three devout Mansunites put their heads through Stove's bass amp. On another, an out-of-control fanatic jumped onstage and, presumably for affectionate reasons, smashed Paul in the teeth with his own mike stand. In Newcastle the fans even attempted to throttle the entire band after leaping onstage. Few other bands attract this curious form of kill the ones you love fan worship. So why Mansun?

Draper attempted to explain to the NME . 'We seem to attract that kind of mad element. Obsessive death threats and all sorts of crazy shit. There was a guy who said that if we played Reading he would kill us. We though it was fantastic! Brilliant! If someone bothered to hate us that much we must have something.' Always look on the dark side, it's more fun that way, seems to be Paul Draper's motto. 'If you are in a band and you sell ten million albums, it doesn't mean you have got ten million fans. (It does, surely?). It means there are forty million

people who hate you. That's the Mansun view.' Paranoia, is the word. Not a bad fuel for a warped, surreal rock'n'roll band; a band terrified of the audience it inspires. I sense that Mansun would find this an interesting concept.

In October, Mansun, finally believing themselves to be ready for a major bout of recording, went into Parr Street and Wessex recording studios in London, where they slammed down the existential classic Wide Open Space. The speed of their studio work may be signified by the fact that, between the recording of this EP and the shooting of the Wide Open Space video (on location in Acton, West London three weeks later), the band had already checked into Mayfair Studios in Primrose Hill to begin sessions on their debut album and had found the time to undertake a short and somewhat portentous Japanese promo tour. Also, before the November release of Wide Open Space, the band slotted in a brief and riotous five-day UK tour.

As Wide Open Space became the most played song on British radio during the period before the Christmas run-in, a Parlophone spokesman was heard muttering, 'I think we have got the hardest working band in Britain.'

This rare touch of artist back-slapping, which surfaced in an otherwise non-related Music Week news story, indicates the true moment when the record company truly began to start wondering about the enormity of Mansun's potential. Until that point the band had been surging along in a post-Britpop state of euphoria but hadn't quite managed to escape the shadows of the larger acts – Oasis, Pulp, Blur et al. But Wide Open Space, with its relentless punch and its supreme confidence, seemed strongly reminiscent of peak period U2. And, in record-company eyes, a lucrative vision of stadium rock would suddenly unfold.

Just in case the band might be charged with in-studio apathy, the band emerged in December to fulfil a largely unnecessary support stint with Sleeper.

The album was mixed and the release of Wide Open Space neatly closed a packed year. Mansun had gone from being the subject of A & R buzz to being generally regarded as one of Britain's established bands. The boys might have been forgiven for treading water for a couple of months, holidaying perhaps, or simply slipping away for a little essential rest. Not so. A fifth EP, topped by lead track, She Makes My Nose Bleed, punched its way into the top ten (the band's first appearance at such a dizzying altitude). The subsequent Top Of The Pops and TFI Friday appearances were, naturally, surrounded by gigs in Amsterdam and Brussels.

As She Makes My Nose Bleed slid down the charts, leaving a shadow of familiarity, Mansun could briefly settle back and ride the momentum. The album release was imminent and touring as support to Suede seemed like the perfect marriage. Suede, with their shabby intelligent glamour and street romance, would be the closest any band could ever come to Mansun's surreal pop glam vision. Like Suede, Mansun could justifiably view themselves as a band apart. Neither band seemed comfortable within the pages of the NME no matter how gushing the superlatives. There was always something spiky there, a sense that they just didn't fit the mould. Mansun and Suede – a marriage made in fishnet heaven.

The gig at Guildford Civic Hall was typical. An excitable, feisty crowd, hungry for barbed pop songs, for a plastic glam that extends back past Morrissey's vision, to the New York Dolls and, ultimately, Ziggy Stardust.

'Exhibitionism's back, isn't it,' Paul Draper proclaimed in Q Magazine. And he was right. In Guildford, that day at least, exhibitionism was well and truly back.

Down Guildford High Street they sauntered that afternoon. Draper resplendent in a striking dogtooth suit, his features punctuated by baby blue eye liner, his nails darkened to Prussian blue. Funnier still, perhaps, was Chad; his frilly shirt billowing forth like blancmange, his thighs clasped in leather jeans tucked neatly into Doc Martins.

'I love going into town like this,' Chad told Q Magazine's Martin Aston. 'People look at you but you never get any hassle. I've always loved dressing up but being in a band gives you licence for all this. . . I've found that wearing nail varnish on one hand is good. But I should start wearing it on my chord-playing hand because it shows up more.'

The upmarket image of the quiffed and suited Draper made an abrupt and, some might say, welcome change from his period spent in orange boiler suits, sporting a flopped haircut plucked directly from an early Blur promo photo. Back then, Mansun might almost have slotted rather too neatly into place, in image if not in music. But Mansun never wanted to fit.

Chad. 'How we look is our vision of what classic pop should be about. I wish being in a band was all just about music, but it's a million other things, all of which can get out of control. It gives you a lot of different avenues to play with and it's important to use them. Any old T-shirt and jeans just won't do.'

ATTACK OF THE GREY LANTERN

[The idea was to make a classic British rock album.]

With no sense of unifying lyrical theme, other than the weird town Draper'sville – in which the deranged, deadly and bizarre characters of Draper's songwriting might reside – it was decided that the album should sweep majestically from the hi-fi, each track melting into a chaotic undertone, before the whole sound would rise again and again. In short, the production would attempt to segue Draper's disparate little stories together, to produce one, unifying sound. The familiar weirdos who inhabited the previously released songs, now seemed to have calmed down a little. Stripper Vicar and his alter ego, Dark Mavis, melted into the background, Egg Shaped Fred seemed meeker and the bondage linked She Makes My Nose Bleed seemed softer. All were mutated into

We made Led Zeppelin seem like Christmas-time advocaat drinkers

'Mansound'. Could this bring with it the ominous charge of over-production?

It would be an easy mistake to make. What might sound lush and vibrant in the studio could so easily emerge, on poor quality CD players up and down the country, as plain dull or unforgivably pompous. In the music business, it is known as 'Tears For Fears syndrome'. The art of using a mixing desk to crush the spark and vivacity out of a songwriter!

Mansun might have taken the opposite tack; to record their songs in with live, spiky, pared down feel. As a first album, this would surely have been admirable, if unadventurous. But the idea was to be bigger. To be large going massive.

Paul Draper. 'We always said from day one that we were not indie. We are not some cult band. We always wanted to be a big group. I'm sure if we had fallen on our arses we would still say we wanted to be a big group. People always namecheck the same bands. Small cult bands – The Stooges, the Velvets, which is great. We are into them too. But we are also into the big bands. The big performers. And we tell people that. So we always say REM, U2. . . that's the level we are aiming at. No point then in making an album that can't make it on that scale is it? Attack Of The Grey Lantern sounds like a massive record. . . and one day it will be. It's like a second album, anyway. Because, when we started we had a publishing deal, we just started banging tracks out. So we already recorded and released 25 tracks before we came to this. . . so we skipped that rough, edgy first album bit.

There are a million guys who would die to be in a big group but they just wouldn't dare admit it

'Actually, we tried to sign to an indie label but we found that there weren't any,' Paul told the NME . 'People turned up at our gigs but they were always the same guys from major labels. Then we looked back at all the bands we thought were boss over the years and thought, God, they are all on major labels. From the Pistols to Bowie to Led Zeppelin to The Who. . . and, at the end of the day it's such a shit way to rebel just by hating your record company. There are a million guys who would die to be in a big group but they just wouldn't dare admit it. They should fucking come out and say it. We said it when we were nothing. That is another thing this album is about. Being big. Rising to your potential. A positive thing.'

Attack Of The Grey Lantern? People had filed the CD neatly away in their record collection without bothering to ask some fairly rudimentary questions. I certainly did. Allowing it to soundtrack the living room for a month, letting it seep into the background before glancing at the sleeve and gamely wondering, so what exactly is a Grey Lantern?

I have never been in love. I've never even really thought about it or ever really want to be in love. To me it's just not that important

It would have been more precise to ask, who is it? The Grey Lantern in question is a Mansun superhero who flits around their heads and songs and is apparently omnipresent throughout their working lives. Live with him, love him, the Grey Lantern is everywhere. Simple? Well, yes, except that this superhero was originally green. Profoundly green. And the album sleeve would have reflected that greenness had they not, at the last minute, switched the superhero's colour to grey. Not that the album sleeve is grey either but don't expect any traces of logic here. Grey became the colour.

Chad. 'Green, we suddenly thought, is a shite colour. Ditch the green. . . so we thought – grey?' Paul. 'I like grey. Chad likes grey. We have this rented house and painted the whole thing grey. Skirting boards, walls, everything. . . got heavily into grey and then realized, it has always been me. I used to wear white T-shirts and they would get dirty very quickly, and become grey. I wore black T-shirts and they would get dandruff and things on them so. . . everything naturally mutated to grey. I'm a logical person. I realized I couldn't fight this creeping greyness. I now wear grey T-shirts and the Lantern. . . well, he's grey.'

But he used to be green!

It took a while to sink in. The album was quietly a classic and very much up there with the greats of 1997 – Radiohead's OK Computer, that Blur album, Primal Scream's Vanishing Point, Verve's Urban Hymns and Prodigy's Fat Of The Land. The sound was cleverly intended to sit at the back of the speakers, gradually enveloping the room, spinning Draper's witticisms here and there.

The album begins beautifully, with the strings of Chad's enchanting intro leading effortlessly into the driven angst of The Chad Who Loved Me

If Elvis or Bill Haley had started off singing about vicars and chickens then maybe everyone would be doing it today

which slowly eases the tempo up a gear, into a kind of tempered attack which continues across the entire album.

There are no love songs, of course. Not even Mansun's Only Love Song which, because of its biting sarcasm, can't possibly be considered. Is Draper, therefore, a man of ice? A detached, dispassionate observer lacking warmth? Lacking soul, even? Or worse, a man naively lost in laddish rock'n'roll mentality?

'I don't think so. . . ' he would claim. 'But it's true that I have never been in love. I've never even really thought about it or ever really want to be in love. To me it's just not that important. Maybe I'll change my mind and be struck by a thunderbolt and start writing loads of sickly stuff. No. I won't. It won't affect me like that. I just feel that there have been too many love songs. Love songs everywhere clogging up real creativity. . . to be honest, I just wanna do something different. If Elvis or Bill Haley had started off singing about

vicars and chickens then maybe everyone would be doing it today – Hard Days Egg or Jailhouse Vicar – and then, maybe, I'd be writing about love. For now, I'm happy basing my character in an imaginary computerized village. . . full of nutters, basically.'

Taxloss, of course, takes irony to a different level, taking a symbolic stab at The Beatles and all they didn't stand for while lampooning the relationship between band and fans. Then again, it's such a genuinely funny song that even those fans washed in blind adoration for the band will surely stand back and wonder just what is going on here. Wide Open Space, of course, is a vast existential desert and, perhaps, a statement of sheer confidence for a songwriter believing himself to be almost peerless?

The singles, Wide Open Space, Stripper Vicar, She Makes My Nose Bleed and Egg Shaped Fred, are scattered evenly over the next 30 minutes of the album, coated in a new production gloss.

The effortless, shady feel then crashes to a sombre halt with the moody Dark Mavis, in which we revisit our garment-shedding clergyman.

Between the tracks is an aural sealant – bells, crying babies, barking dogs – sounds produced not by the studio computer, but by Draper's archaic '60s Mellotron. A kind of synthesizer, used in the days before synthesizers existed, even back in the early '60s few bands saw their potential. They were mainly used as effects instruments in TV plays, which is a shame because, as Draper perceptively realized, the Mellotron produces a warmness of sound that no computer can compete with. It's just a small touch but one that brings an earthiness to the recordings.

Paul Draper's Mellotron would sit in his kitchen, in a state of post-album disrepair, for most of 1997. Draper would attempt to restore it, every now and again, like some weekend hobbyist restoring a rusting bicycle. Watch out for the Mellotron's poetic effects re-emerging on future Mansun releases.

The album was launched, somewhat perversely, on the Isle of Man. Its touristic allure has faded, but it is still, somehow, a symbolic, secret place, known to holidaymakers from the north-west of England and generally a mystery to those in the south. The location was chosen with this in mind, as a feint slap in the face to the London-based music business who found it a difficult, irritating little trip. For Mansun, the short hop across the Irish sea brought back memories of childhood holidays.

Depending on your point of view, the little promotional soireé was either a triumph or disaster. It climaxed in glass smashing, drink throwing, table smashing and a mock ruck which, not surprisingly, twisted into a serious disturbance as aggrieved locals forged into the fray. The poor Stakis Casino staff could only watch and weep as Mansun's own tour manager single-handedly ripped the bar apart.

Although superficially enraged by the behaviour of what was still just a 'happening' act, Parlophone soon dropped their veneer of indignation when,against all the odds, Attack Of The Grey Lantern knocked the superb album by their label mates, Blur, from the top spot after just one week of release. Blur, quite rightly, had been given the full promotional treatment and although expectations weren't as high as for their previous more commercial album, three weeks at the top was certainly anticipated. Mansun might edge into the top five one week later.

It wasn't the lack of Blur sales that caused the shock, it was the unexpected clamour for Mansun product. More commercial, it now seemed, than anyone could have expected. 'That's true,' agreed Paul Draper. 'We were just as surprised as everyone else by that. I mean we knew we were growing fast, but until the record's out there, you just can't tell. I'd have been happy with a top ten album at that point. After all, it was only a year after we started, really. . . and back then were genuinely perceived, and quite correctly as a bunch of no copyist no hopers.'

Video director Roman Copolla – son of Godfather director Francis Ford Copolla – had fun when presented with the rather clear and sarcastic Taxloss. As the song was loosely aimed at Beatles-style pop star cavorting, he decided to nod back to KLF's stunning artistic wheeze, to burn £1 million. This would be a little more modest. A mere £25,000 would be dispensed and, unlike the awesome pointlessness of the KLF scam, at least some people would benefit. They would be the point of it all. The idea was for £25,000 to be scattered from the balcony of Liverpool Street Station, causing a hilarious furore amongst the hapless commuters, trudging in from Essex to work in the city. Although the notion of chucking away £25,000, merely for effect, might seem appallingly rash, and not at all in keeping with record-company practice in 1997, it would be considerably cheaper than flying the band to a Caribbean island to perfect close ups. The whole scam would be filmed swiftly, using little more than video footage. In fact the Taxloss video was surprisingly cheap for a band of Mansun's stature.

The filming was simple. A hurried pre-scam meeting, followed by a little tester scene where one £5 note is placed on the concourse. The camera then zooms in on the face of the accomplice of the man who picks it up and then five men in black storm to the balcony, hurling fivers into the air, showering them down on the unsuspecting commuters.

After a minute or so of stony-faced confusion, the concourse was transformed into a mass scurry. Moving cleverly and hilariously in tandem with the song Chad's guitar picks up the pace. Following a couple of close ups, of embarrassed people scrambling around on the concourse floor, the video fades to leave the disembodied voice of a GLR newsreader. '. . . at Liverpool Street Station today, where rock band Mansun were filming a video and scattering £25,000 across the concourse. . . Railtrack were furious, stating that the scam could have caused injuries. However, they later admitted that they had not received one single complaint.'

Draper later declared that he would have loved to wander invisibly through the EMI boardroom after the band's proposition to chuck away £25,000 was initially discussed. 'They smiled and agreed and thought it was a really wonderful idea and told us how great we were. . . but I bet they were gritting their teeth. Wouldn't have blamed them, actually, but I would have loved to have been behind the scenes.' Ⓜ

C H A P T E R   S I X

THE HONG KONG AFFAIR

['No relation...we are no relation to any other bands,' stated Draper, in a forthright and somewhat portentous interview.]

In Hong Kong's largest circulation English language paper, The South China Morning and throughout Asia, the scattered and disparate music press seemed to be wilting, somewhat, under a barrage of pre-tour reports that would have been reasonable coverage for a new U2 or Simply Red tour. The tour, which would sway through Australia, Japan, South Korea, Malaysia – where they had apparently already attained demi-god status – and Hong Kong, was solidly preceded by a wave of articles spiked by an unusually aggressive Draper.

MANSUN

62

There was certain consternation too, among music loving ex-pats in Japan and Hong Kong who, some way behind the hype of Britain it must be said, were still clinging fervently to an overt fondness for Morrissey and The Smiths. The Oasis invasion had carried with it large amount of retrospective fondness for The Smiths and The Beatles and it seemed odd to hear a lone voice – from Chester – talking down such influence.

'Is Morrissey a good songwriter then?' quipped Draper before adding, 'I haven't got a single Smiths record.' Whether this was off-the-cuff sarcasm or not remains difficult to judge but the question seemed to be significant. Perhaps we have entered a truly new era. At any time during the previous decade, the thought of a modern, clever, witty songwriter and band leader openly stating that he has no idea whether Morrissey is a good songwriter or not, would seem to indicate, at the very least, a gaping hole in the new star's credibility, such was the esteem heaped on Mozzer and Marr's gang. But that shadow of influence may now have gone.

'Can't say anything about The Smiths,' continued Draper, 'but we've been compared to everyone from The Cranberries to U2 to Radiohead. Blur is the latest. We are also a cross between the Manic Street Preachers and Tears for Fears. But it's a critics job to compare and a musician's job to deny them.'

On the subject of Hong Kong, Draper seemed to have no reservations at all. 'I don't know much about Hong Kong but I can't wait to go. I'd love to be the last British band to play there on June 30th.'

> (Mansun) don't even look like they belong in the same decade as each other, never mind the same band

Stephen Dalton, *NME*

She was to become infamous, symbolic even. A pouting Japanese fan, a shock of orange hair and penetrating eyes. In photographs which peppered the British music press she could be seen clutching Paul Draper. Not a hint of distress clouds her eyes. Her short, frayed shorts are barely covered by a black Kurt Cobain Obituary T-shirt. On Mansun's short stint to Japan, they had encountered a level of fan worship on a scale that left them genuinely stunned. The girl had attached herself to the band, becoming a symbol of the comparatively incident-free trek around Japan's pristine halls of rock'n'roll.

There was no sign that there might be anything slightly odd about the girl. Although she was obsessive in a hero-worshipping intense way that, thankfully, no longer affects bands like Mansun in the west, her behaviour hadn't seemed beyond the bounds of rationality.

But after Mansun's final gig in Tokyo, things changed. Half the band and crew, plus a couple of dozen eager girlies, fell from the city's neat, ordered streets into The Milk Club, a pulsating drum'n'bass cellar club. It seemed that all the criminals, prostitutes and dubious types who, in any western city, would be prowling the streets, were involved in a cheek-by-jowl mass rave. The NME would later describe the club as

'something straight out of A Clockwork Orange'. All neon and menace, piercing stares and cocktails; acres of female flesh and Armani suits. Rather aptly for Mansun though, it seemed to be a club teetering on the verge of absurdity, a fact highlighted by the giant snapshot of Simon Le Bon which glared glumly down from above the spiral staircase.

Mansun wandered glassy-eyed into this unlikely environment, a solid unit, shutting out the rest of the world. Including, it seems, the Japanese girl in the Nirvana T-shirt who, after failing to capture the attention of Chad and Andy, took a Stanley Knife out of her bag, rolled back her sleeves to reveal the words Maralyn Mansun carved across both forearms in scar tissue, and proceeded to hack away at her exposed flesh. The shocked Mansun party fell back into a semicircle, with an angered Andy Rathbone storming from the scene. Chad, however, helped stem the flow of blood, showering the girl in sympathy which presumably, had been her goal for the entire sojourn. One day later the girl, apparently in good health and full of regret, had unwittingly achieved a certain notoriety as two British tabloids reported and, naturally, exaggerated the incident until the story resembled the script of Play Misty For Me.

Chad managed to get a sense of perspective into the incident. 'It was just a bit of stupidity in a nightclub. She was just a kid, really. . . looking for attention. I think she learned something from it. . . she seemed quite genuine afterwards.'

The girl wasn't typical of the Japanese fans – most of whom seemed happy to moon about hotel lobbies, hoping for a glimpse of someone famous from the western world – but she did serve as a reminder of how such worship can quickly escalate. 'We are aware of that,' said

We do know what fans, especially obsessed female fans, are capable of. It's really frightening in one sense but, I must say, nearly all of them are really sweet

Is Morrissey a good songwriter then? I haven't got a single Smiths record

Paul Draper

Stove, 'I mean, it still seems a bit odd to us. . . but we do know what fans. . . and especially obsessed female fans, are capable of. It's really frightening in one sense but, I must say, nearly all of them are really sweet'.

As Mansun wandered through the Shibuya, Tokyo's upbeat modernistic shopping complex, it was noted that their appearance might seem confusing to locals, not too clued into their rock'n'roll fads and fashions guide book. Stephen Dalton from the NME mentioned that the Mansun crowd '. . . don't even look like they belong in the same decade as each other, never mind the same band.'

A reasonable statement, as Paul was wearing bondage trousers and a polar fleece. Chad was garbed in a space-age jumpsuit and suede dog tags. Andy sported a leather pimp greatcoat and tartan flares while Stove favoured full Edwardian hippie garb. With respect to Japanese rock fans, who are undoubtedly blessed with a greater sense of irony than we give them credit for, the signals sent by such pick'n'mix imagery must have been unsettling. At first glance they might seem to be little more than a glittery caricature, rather like John Robb's shamelessly flash Gold Blade. Then again as Draper's songwriting would begin to unfold with all its magpie cheek, perhaps such an open dress code might begin to make

In the simplistic world of the British

enough to sink the band to the catego

of that rather less intelligent, monum

perfect sense. . . even to the Japanese!

By this time Mansun were beginning to become used to 'on-tour incidents' Barely a day would pass without something going horribly wrong, or terribly well. Sometimes both. In Australia they caused a determined 20-staff walkout from a television station after performing 20 decibels louder than the union maximum. And this was a rock show that had previously featured AC/DC! Mind you, the band themselves stormed out of a recording for Malaysian TV when, bizarrely, Chad's admittedly unkempt blond mop top was deemed illegal

under a severe local law. Worst still, from the band's point of view, was the discovery that all their singles had been banned by Malaysian radio because of their religious content. Presumably the dark humour of Stripper Vicar didn't translate too well. Added to this was the curious fact that the venue they had been supposed to be playing, that night, had been firebombed to prevent some second rate, local western rock copyist band from performing their evil act. Maybe it was the taste terrorists?

But the true highlight of Mansun's eastern madness was surely Hong Kong where, in the

oids, one smashed hotel room was

of the two-fingered yob mentality

lly successful outfit from Burnage

Hard Rock Cafe, they had sparked a mini riot. The gig, for Hong Kong radio, came hot on the heels of a Suede performance at the same venue which, apparently, had given the local kids a taste for audience participation. As such, the performance was fairly wild but not, according to the band, uncontrollable. Until the band left the stage. Tired of being pushed back by a line of bouncers who had no idea how to control a western-style rock concert. The kids suddenly rebelled blasting their way through the bouncers and the TV cameras, the stage and the equipment. Everything came crashing

down in a rather flattering orgy of destruction.

The local press saw it differently. Oliver Poole, reporting for the South China Morning, noted, 'A performance by top British pop group Mansun descended into a punch-up between the lead singer and security guards. Paul Draper threw a speaker off the stage and smashed a microphone system in front of 500 cheering fans at the Hard Rock Cafe on Saturday night. When staff at the Tsim Sha Tsui restaurant rushed to restrain the 23-year old he attacked them. Scuffles then broke out among the audience. Yesterday the chain's entertainment

manager Jacky Chan Chun-kit said about $500 of damage had been done. "The singer kicked and hit me," he said. "I have never seen a band behave like that".

'Only a plea from EMI, the group's record company, prevented the police from being called. The restaurant chain has now banned the group on their first visit to the territory and from all its outlets worldwide. The group have huge support in Britain where their album, Attack Of The Grey Lantern went to number one. Yessterday band members were unavailable for comment. EMI's marketing manager Kevin Wong-Kin-ho blamed the brawl on the group becoming swept away with the music. The band leaves for Japan today.'

There was more. The band, perhaps inspired by the unlikely ferocity of their audience in Hong Kong, returned to the hotel and started to wreck their rooms.

Paul Draper. 'We smashed the whole place up. . . but they used this as a propaganda tool. "See we told you this Western influence would be bad for Hong Kong". We were just pawns in their game. We got out of there as quick as possible.'

Just pawns or simply playing naively into the hands of the authorities? Whatever, the actions of Mansun in Hong Kong suddenly alerted the whole big gang of British ex-pat hacks. Mansun wrecking a hotel was simply a big local story, something for the copy-hungry hacks to swiftly fax back to editors in the UK. Something too, for them all to chatter about in the bar of the Foreign Correspondents Club. And the chatter reached just about every national and local newspaper in Britain with Mansun duly tagged as the new bad boys of Brit pop. In the simplistic world of the British tabloids, one smashed hotel room was enough

to sink the band to the category of the two-fingered yob mentality of that rather less intelligent, monumentally successful outfit from Burnage.

'It made a big impact in Hong Kong,' says ex-pat journalist Michael Mackey, who filed the story for an exceptionally hungry Liverpool Echo and later, the Sunday People. '...there was a lot of talk about just why it was taken so seriously. I didn't know who this band were, none of us did, I suspect Draper has an ability to talk provocatively, or at least talk in such a way that he gives good quotes. I initially just filed quotes from an interview with him and I was surprised to find the Liverpool Echo really snatching at the story, any Mansun story. But I thought that would be it, until I opened the South China Morning Post to read about the Hard Rock Cafe incident. This sort of behaviour is unheard of by local and visiting bands. People are always very polite in Hong Kong. Papers from England started phoning me back, really eager, so I thought there was a bit of spin-doctoring going on. That may sound cynical, but it seemed as if some PR company was trying to turn this band into some kind of Sex Pistols thing. The News Of the World were really hot for it but then they dropped it when The Sun ran a piece in their Bizarre column. Why is this interesting? Because, to be honest, this sort of thing doesn't work in Hong Kong. We (journalists) had a feeling that, after this, Mansun would never do as well in Hong Kong as they should. And now, six months later, it is strangely difficult to find a Mansun CD in this city. I may be wrong, and this is just an opinion, but I think they upset a few of the wrong people. I think they are blacklisted.'

THE WORLD'S STILL OPEN

[Back in England, the band supported The Manic Street Preachers at the Nynex Arena, in Manchester.]

In front of 15,000 ecstatic fans, Mansun performed a spirited set. The gig, which caught the Manics at the peak of their Design For Life supremacy, was generally regarded as the finest rock event in the north west during 1997. It can be assumed that the decision to allow Mansun to venture onto that stage was nothing short of inspired. It can't be argued that Mansun blew the Manics offstage – for the headlining act produced a show of simply awesome power – but most people agreed that Mansun were one of the few British bands capable of holding their own in such company.

Significantly, staff at Manchester's Virgin and HMV megastores noted a violent surge in sales of Attack Of The Grey Lantern during the following week. To celebrate, Mansun produced an even more exceptional performance, perhaps the finest of their career to date, at Glasgow's Barrowlands. It was a triumphant period topped, perhaps, by a sublime appearance – two songs, Mansun's Only Love Song and Wide Open Space on the celebrated TV show, Later With Jools Holland.

Paul Draper. 'It was fantastic. . . the Jools Holland thing. For the first time I felt like we had been truly accepted. We were a recognized force. . . that felt good, really good.'

This good feeling remained with the band throughout the summer of 1997 while they toured the festival circuits of Europe and Britain. At the Hurricane Festival in Germany they apparently made numerous fans from a Hells Angels fraternity while at Glastonbury, the band had to abandon their set after just one song when the power supply was overwhelmed by a sea of mud. Despite this the band achieved rave reviews in the following week's music press. Little though, could prepare them for a series of dream dates supporting David Bowie in Italy and Spain. They anticipated a cold, professional, distant relationship with the headliner, they were stunned to discover Bowie to be warm and friendly. He was quite prepared to 'hang out' with the band, mulling over a few beers and chatting about music in general. Bowie seemed to appreciate Mansun's music as well for he was seen swaying in the aisles, soaking in the Mansun stage show. This brief liaison would be celebrated by Draper and Chad who, back in England, famously recreated the Bowie/Ronson onstage antics, plucked directly from the Ziggy Stardust period.

Despite the rigours of such heavy activity, Draper's prolific rate of writing seemed, if anything, to increase.

'I just write all the time – lying in bed, over breakfast, when we are out having beers, on aeroplanes, watching television, it all seems to funnel down to writing. You see, the band is a 100% thing. I don't have any time off because there is no need. I relax by writing, by searching for new ideas, by rehearsing new songs all the time. It's easy for me because I look for absurdities. That's all I do and, it seems, the more I look the more I find. The recent death of Princess Diana was a case in point. What a strange period in British history that was all that mass hysteria. I believe that people are looking for something to replace God. People have lost their spirituality. The world is too small for people to be scared into believing in deities. Before they were terrified into giving their money to the church. It's about aura, but people are deluding themselves. I try to reflect that, in all kinds of strange ways.'

But will Draper's outpourings prove too clever for the average rock fan? A certain simplicity of style such as that eschewed by U2, Simple Minds and Oasis, the cleverest format, just because it doesn't overstate the importance of a rock band?

Draper. 'People are always trying to pin us down. Our critics said at the beginning we were hooligans because we wrecked and smashed things up but we are not louts. I'm not a sensitive artist pouring out his angst either. I believe in pop music and entertainment. . . but I think that our fans do listen to the lyrics, and they do mean something real to them. Most of them have made a conscious decision to get into us. We are not the sort of band that the lads down the pub listen to.'

CHAPTER SEVEN

September 1997

Mansun in Santa Monica. It has an ill-fitting ring to it. Three magazines, including the NME, were on hand to witness this tiny culture shock. Amid the filming of Baywatch on the beaches of Topanga, Carbon and Malibu. Helicopters swirling across the surf. Deeply bronzed and familiar bodies wobbling past delicately posed cameras, flanked by gatherings of bearded technicians and, further out, basking in eternal sadness, the typical American celeb spotters.

And Mansun. Brilliant white gatecrashers from Chester, wandering down the beach. Causing a minor affray. The dark glances they cast, enraged producers who were unaccustomed to having black-denimmed rock bands spoiling the acres of beauty and miles of rather boring beaches that combine to make that ultimate vision of '90s Americana. Baywatch. Never mind the quality, oggle the orbs.

It wasn't lost on the NME or Spin Magazine, for that matter, that Mansun's little invasion is a neat microcosm of their surge into the American music business. They are out of place and out of time but fully aware of the failure of previous English bands, especially those of a rather camp nature, to puncture the US

defences. One is reminded of the spectacular failure of Suede, half a decade previously, when their glorious songwriting was beaten into second place by the allure of the cute, melodic Cranberries, complete with Irish eyes and steely pouts. But if America couldn't get to grips with the intelligence of Brett Anderson, what on earth would they make of the audio-visual cocktail offered by Mansun?

Mansun had been in the USA for one month, providing weighty support for the ascendant Seahorses. By all accounts, Mansun's powerful stage presence had upstaged John Squires' talented but untested troubadours in every town. A feat certainly helped by the fact that America had seemingly understood the existential angst of Wide Open Space and had decided to clutch this strange bunch to its fickle bosom.

To illustrate this, there had even been examples of the song being played in baseball stadiums in celebration of a home run. Almost without trying, the band had, it seemed, created a US-approved modern rock classic. Only Bush, untouchable in America, untouched in Britain could claim to have traversed the barriers with such serene ease.

80

The American experience, however, had been enough to halt the band's drift into sobriety. For a successful tour of America comes complete with a multitude of gaping opportunities for rampant hedonism. And so it was with Mansun.

'I was off me face before we went on. . . pissed as fuck,' spat Paul Draper to the NME's Mark Beaumont. As the tour dates piled up and merged into a messy colourful blur, it seemed impossible to ignore that state of English-band-on-road syndrome. Take Stove. Somehow, somewhere aloong the way, his rear region had attained a large tattoo; a slightly askew vision of Bert and Ernie from Sesame Steet.

. College radio, that vast network of hip, young, gunslinging DJs, grasped Mansun's music with feverish enthusiasm during the tour absurdly proclaiming them to be 'the new U2'. Depending on who you are - a record company person with eyes on the big prize, or Chad, a guitarist with a mission to produce genuinely innovative licks and hooks, this is either hugely flattering or a damning insult. The band remained rather amused though, by the college radio idea that all British (and Irish) bands were somehow interchangeable, and were all living in some tiny rock band community in Devon. ('Oh hi Mansun, hey I met some friends of yours last week, Spice Girls. . . you must know them, they are from Britain. . . ')

Perhaps even more amusing was the DJ who, for reasons only he could know, was clearly convinced that Paul and Chad were in fact called Chas and Dave. Reports suggest that, despite the band's display of indignant disbelief, the DJ still wasn't convinced. The similarity in the names, in his view, was just too much of a coincidence. Creepy.

Back in Britain, in the pages of the Chester Chronicle, in which not surprisingly the band had attained God-like status, Draper wisely decided not to pour out the usual stream of rock star rhetoric. Instead his mood was tinged with guilt.

'We have hopped over the Atlantic a couple of times now and it's difficult to come to terms with. Jet lag is something that lucky bands have to contend with. Although it can be a bit disorientating when you find yourself sound-checking and, just for a moment, you begin wondering just what country you are in. It is a bit mind blowing. I hope that doesn't sound pompous. I'm having the time of me life mate.'

October 1997

To the continued anxiety of their Parlophone A & R man, nobody quite knows what Mansun will do next. This stylized unpredictability has become part and parcel of their deal until they are always expected to produce the unusual; to change their look at the worst possible time; to confound and confuse their fans; to mystify their critics; to send rock journalists scrambling back to the reference books and to shed the kind of casual half-fans who have attached themselves to any particular Mansun single expecting more of the same. This may be little more than commercial suicide but it keeps their marketing department on the edge. How could it be any other way with Mansun? Throughout the autumn of 1997, the triumphant band contrived to step deeper into commercial, as well as artistic perversity.

Full Circle

Howard Devoto had retired. His latterday work with, amongst others, Luxuria, could not manage to attain the ongoing kudos of Magazine, a band who, largely thanks to Mansun, seeped into more open-minded young heads during the course of 1997. Devoto himself is, one strongly senses, fairly bewildered himself. He had been living and working in north London, and had deliberately allowed only one link with the music business to remain – his long-term friendship with Morrissey (though latterly distant), who he had first met at that Levenshulme party, 21 years previously.

Paul Draper had picked up on Magazine, back at school, after borrowing a copy of the band's ground breaking Real Life album from a surprisingly musically knowledgeable friend. It was difficult for him to fall in love with Devoto's lyricism, for the album was deliberately and courageously pretentious, The lyrics were lush, sweeping and absurd. They seemed to be from a different planet. But they were also laced with a vicious socially aware wit which suggested that Devoto was playing a few mind games with his listeners. This trickery can be traced back to his lyrics on The Buzzcocks' stunning and cheaply produced debut disc, Spiral Scratch.

Draper has obviously learned a great deal from Devoto. How to place lyrical complexity over a simplistic backbeat; the use of overt sarcasm and tongue-in-cheek pomposity. All are Devoto trademarks which can now be found in abundance throughout Mansun's rapidly expanding repertoire.

Age-old Magazine fans, Mansun contacted Devoto through a mutual friend and although initially he showed nothing more than weary reluctance, he warmed to the idea of some kind of collaboration after sitting down and soaking in Mansun's recorded output. He was doubtless also rather flattered that such a young band had openly cited him as a major influence.

After a few meetings a friendship began to develop and Devoto started sending lyrics to the band. He followed this with a few chord structures which the band, eager for a new twist, began immediately working on. They tentatively sent their interpretations back to him. Soon the track Everyone Must Win, with its echoes of new-wave circa Magazine and The Skids, began to take form. This collaboration seemed to be working so well that two more tracks were duly recorded as well as a Mansun cover of an unreleased Devoto song called Railings. Although he agreed to provide vocals on Everyone Must Win, Devoto refused to be drawn out into public appearance. Nevertheless,

Lennon and McCartney released 200 (songs) in eight years, so I'm writing at twice their rate. I've got so many ideas, it's not a problem. I thrive on being creative

Paul Draper

the band remained hopeful that he would be contributing to future recordings, if nothing else, on guitar.

To Mansun's collective delight, when Devoto arrived at the studio he turned out to be inspirational. Draper was eager to learn the differences between performing and producing and quickly accepted Devoto's advice when the ex-Magazine man pulled him away from the desk. 'Sometimes,' explained Devoto, 'it's better to non-produce, to move away, record quickly, let the musicianship flow naturally.'

It worked, too, as Mansun came to accept the Devoto notion that recording in one take, while drunk, will nine times out of ten, produce better results than sitting around endlessly arguing about effects, overdubs and drum sounds Interestingly enough, the Closed For Business EP, although rather eccentric, is fired by a notably fresher feel than the album.

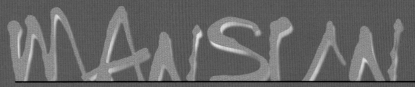

Closed For Business was hyped by the reports of the liaison with Howard Devoto. Yet what other band, on the brink of worldwide success, would choose to open the all-important post hit-album release in such a strange and eerie way. A lilting harpsichord refrain dips into a disorientating guitar break which makes way for a disarmingly haunting melody. All too soon it is replaced by the harsh Holidays In the Sun style blast of marching feet and a psychotic poem. It must be said that the reserved melody of Closed For Business does sit beneath a lyric so packed with sheer vehemence, it wouldn't disgrace an Oi band.

One has visions of Parlophone reps across the country cradling their heads in their hands, wondering just how they could possibly plug this! It is such a relief then to hear the distant familiarity of Howard Devoto, engagingly whining through Everyone Must Win. And then, perched in the shadows at the tail-end of the CD, comes The World's Still Open. A song that the NME quite correctly, regarded as a 'sure fire number one smash hit everywhere from Telford to Tibet. . . if it wasn't at the end.'

Paul Draper. 'The last thing I give a shit about is commercialism or the charts or the radio or having a hit single. A few people said The World Is Still Open is a big hit but I don't want to just have hit singles. When we finished them four tracks, the one we thought was the most innovative was Closed For Business. So we decided that's what should represent the whole EP on radio. Chad's playing a harpsichord on it, it's in waltz time and it's two-and-a-half minutes long. There's not many bands prepared to stick their necks on the line and do a two-and-a-half minute harpsichord waltz and put it out as their first single after the album. The worst thing you can do is to play safe.'

Dangerous words. All too reminiscent of the warped logic of progressive rock, where talented musicians were forced to hide their most supreme melodies behind a veil of musicianly introversion. It was almost true, back then, that behind every dull and pompous prog rock band, a vivacious hit factory was struggling to get out. More fool them. Could Mansun be heading the same way? Could they be allowing their musicianly wanderings to pull them away from the desires of their fan base? Perhaps not, but the danger signs were there. After all, this was not the first time that Mansun chose to hide away their true gems.

Paul Draper. 'When this band's over there will be some amazing lost tracks there. All our singles have been deleted. You won't be able to get hold of those tracks and I like that.'

The point of this escapes this particular writer unless we are willing to run with the curious notion that Mansun are like an iceberg. Their most impressive mass, laying submerged. A secret for their fans to share, intensifying the feeling of belonging to a club. The problem is, this doesn't quite square with the day-to-day mechanical workings of a highly prolific band who are committed to conquering the world.

Strangely, this spat of commercial weirdness could well have worked in the band's favour, for Closed For Business broke the track-to-track 'boom' of British daytime radio with reassuring success, drawing attention to the song from listeners and DJs alike, mostly along the lines of, '. . . they are a really unusual band, Mansun, aren't they. . . ' In these days of multiple 'clone bands', this, itself, was surely praise.

The EP, incidentally, took just nine days to record, mix and deliver. Parlophone must, by now, have realized that they had a dream band on their hands here. No five-year drug sojourns,

no negative bickering, no sitting back and basking in celebrity. Mansun, a full-on writing recording and gigging unit.

Just as controversial was the decision to wrap their music in the paintings of Stuart Sutcliffe. It was the first time, that any band had been granted permission to use the late ex-Beatle's work. As Sutcliffe remains eternally wrapped in a state of enigma it has been argued that Mansun were simply credibility grasping. Draper is quick to deny this:

'Stuart Sutcliffe is a historical figure who painted some great paintings. That combination made us ask for the cover. If the paintings were

shit we wouldn't have them on, but they are actually quite good. Anything that gets the kids into anything except fucking Nintendo or opens people's eyes to a bit of culture, opens peoples' eyes to Stuart Sutcliffe or anything, is good.'

Mansun's Top Of the Pops appearance, screened on Friday 17 October 1997, clearly showed the curious paradoxes surrounding the band. Presenter Jayne Middlemiss was swept aside to reveal a band performance which, visually at least, looked more like Nazareth at Sheffield City Hall in 1972 than the 1997 TOTP norm. It was all lights and fire flashes, with an audience comprising of waves of wormlike waving arms. A snippet of Mansun in concert. and then, of course, Closed For Business, which seemed quite unfathomable in this setting, with its slowing pace, anguished vocals and choppy guitar. Could this be the same set that, just six minutes later, would be playing house to the perfect complex choreography of Janet Jackson and the hairy whimsy of Supergrass?

But the near-hysterical girls didn't seem to care; they merely surged with a vigour rarely seen on Top Of The Pops these days. And there, in an instant, we could see the true Mansun paradox. Ever since Attack Of The Grey Lantern started picking up serious music press reviews, the surreal nature of the band's songwriting had started to attract a new fan base derived mainly from Radiohead fans searching for new progressive angles to partner their main obsession. There is little doubt that Attack Of The Grey Lantern is the perfect complementary partner to Radiohead's OK Computer. Both contain moments of surprising delicacy and both are firmly locked inside worlds of their own. But Mansun, as this Top Of The Pops appearance so clearly demonstrated, are also, undeniably something else. They are young, good looking and seem far too innocent to be making music of such depth. At first glance this looks like a teen pop outfit.

There are, at present, a number of Mansun fanzines circulating and Mansun fall almost equally on both sides of the divide. Teen-zines say '. . . nothing wrong with them,' or sway into articles about Paul Draper's trousers, eyes and wit while attempting, with varying degrees of success, serious critical appraisal. It is difficult to think of another band who can successfully ride such a divide. Teen pop bands can't usually cross over to make serious or rockier music, although there have been many attempts.

But is this a problem? Well, it might be, if Mansun are too awesomely prolific, so wholly dedicated to ploughing their own furrow.

For instance, the EP (the seventh in two years), racked up the number of recorded Mansun songs to an astonishing 36. Almost all of them coming from the unstoppable Draper. Should they continue at this rate, and all the signs are that, despite record company pressure to slow down, Mansun will, by the close of 1998, have released 80 songs. On the global stadium rock circuit, one album and one tour every four years is the average.

Draper proudly mused over this fact in the Times Metro Magazine.

'Lennon and McCartney released 200 in eight years, so I'm writing at twice their rate. I've got so many ideas, it's not a problem. I thrive on being creative.'

So much so, that, before the EP had even reached the shops and while the band were touring the UK, Draper was already scribbling down lyrics, running ideas past the rest of the band, feverishly readying himself for the recording of the band's next album.

Draper. 'I don't want the next record to sound anything like Grey Lantern. . . we are just going to piss into the wind and whatever comes out, comes out. I've run out of fucking hairstyles now, so it's time to change the music.'

With Mansun, it is always time to change the music.

GIGOGRAPHY

1995
November

8th	Dundee, Westpoint
9th	Edinburgh University
10th	Leeds, Brighton Beach
14th	Birmingham, Jug Of Ale
15th	Middlesborough, Corner House
16th	Newport TJ's
17th	Wolverhampton, Civic Hall (supporting The Charlatans)
18th	Essex University (supporting The Charlatans)
20th	Exeter, Cavern
21st	Southampton, Guild Hall (supporting The Charlatans)
22nd	Southampton, Joiners Arms
23rd	Bath, Moles Club
24th	Harlow Square
25th	Brixton Academy (supporting The Charlatans)
29th	Buckley, Tivoli
30th	Stoke, The Stage

December

1st	Hull, Adelphi
2nd	Sheffield, Leadmill

1996
Audioweb Tour
February

20th	Norwich UEA
21st	Bristol, Louisiana
22nd	Liverpool, Lomax
24th	Wolverhampton Varsity
26th	Leeds, Duchess Of York
27th	Manchester University
28th	Edinburgh, Venue
29th	Loughborough University

March

1st	London, The Garage
2nd	Coventry University
3rd	Southampton, Joiner's Arms
5th	Brighton University

Shed Seven Tour
April

17th	Newcastle University
18th	Glasgow, The Plaza
19th	Edinburgh, Queens Hall
1st	Hull, Tower Ballroom
22nd	Leicester, De Montford University
23rd	Northampton, Roadmenders
24th	Sheffield University
26th	Manchester University
27th	Wolverhampton, Wulfrun Hall
28th	Nottingham, Rock City
29th	Cambridge, Junction

May

1st	Bristol University
2nd	Portsmouth, Pyramids
3rd	London, Shepherds Bush Empire
4th	London, Forum

Headlining Tour
June

3rd	Manchester University
4th	Newcastle, Riverside
5th	Buckley, Tivoli
6th	Bath, Moles
8th	Hastings, Crypt
10th	Bristol, Fleece and Firkin
11th	London, Tabernacle
12th	Portsmouth, Wedgewood Rooms
13th	Bedford, Esquires
15th	Sheffield, Leadmill
16th	Hull, Adelphi
17th	Southampton, Joiners Arms
18th	Tunbridge Wells, Forum (gig cancelled)
20th	Stoke, The Stage
21st	Leeds, Brighton Beach
22nd	Oxford, Zodiac
30th	Aberdeen, Pelican Club

July

1st	Dundee University

Headlining Tour
August

22nd	Leicester, Charlotte
23rd	Newcastle, Riverside

92

28th	Reading, Alleycat
29th	Oxford, Zodiac
30th	Tunbridge Wells, Forum
31st	Chelmsford, Y Club

September

3rd	Norwich, Arts Centre
4th	Stoke, The Stage
6th	Doncaster, Leopard Club
7th	York, Fibbers
10th	Middlesborough, Cornerhouse
11th	Glasgow, King Tut's Wah Wah Hut
12th	Aberdeen, Pelican Club
13th	Dundee, West Port Bar
14th	Edinburgh, Venue
17th	Hull, Adelphi
18th	Cheltenham, Axiom
19th	Wolverhampton, Varsity
21st	Manchester, Roadhouse
22nd	Brighton, Concorde
24th	Southampton, Joiner's Arms
25th	Plymouth, Cooperage
26th	Bath, Moles Club
27th	Exeter, Cavern
28th	Blackwood, Miner's Institute

November

12th	London, Astoria
	Soho Live Festival
	(supporting Super Furry Animals)

Headlining Tour
November

25th	Glasgow, King Tut's Wah Wah Hut
26th	London, 100 Club
27th	Bristol, Fleece
28th	Portsmouth, Wedgewood
30th	Wolverhampton, Varsity

Supporting Sleeper
December

2nd	Watford, Colosseum
3rd	Gloucester, Leisure Centre
4th	Aston Villa, Leisure Centre
7th	Middlesborough, Town Hall
8th	Leeds, Town and Country Club
9th	Derby, Assembley Rooms
11th	Torquay, Riviera Centre

12th	Plymouth, Guildhall
13th	Guildford, Civic Hall
14th	Ilford, Island

1997
January

17th	Amsterdam Milky Way Club
	(headlining)

Suede Tour
January

26th	Bradford, St Georges
27th	Poole Arts Centre
28th	Guildford, Civic Hall
30th	Cambridge, Corn Exchange

February

3rd	Brighton Centre
4th	Folkestone Leas Cliff Hall
5th	Reading, Rivermead
7th	Plymouth, Pavilions
8th	Watford, Colosseum
9th	York, Barbican (gig cancelled)
11th	Middlesborough, Town Hall
13th	Edinburgh, Usher Hall
14th	Carlisle, Sands Centre
15th	Blackburn, King Georges Hall

Attack Of The Grey Lantern Tour
February

17th.	Douglas, Bushes Casino

March

1st	Aberdeen, Lemon Tree
2nd	Edinburgh, Venue
3rd	Newcastle, Riverside
4th	Middlesborough, Town Hall
6th	Manchester University
7th	Leeds, Brighton Beach
8th	Northampton, Roadmender
9th	Cambridge, Junction
11th	Norwich, Waterfront
12th	Reading, Alleycat
14th	Oxford, Zodiac
17th	Bristol University
18th	Brighton Centre, East Wing
19th	Exeter University

MANISPAN

GIGOGRAPHY

Far East and Australia.
April
3rd	Australia.	Sydney, The Metro
4th	Australia.	Melbourne, Cornerhouse
16th	Japan.	Tokyo, Quattro Club
17th	Japan.	Tokyo, Quattro Club
19th	Japan.	Osaka, Quattro Club
20th	Japan.	Nagoya, Quattro Club

Taxloss Tour
April
24th	Wolverhampton, Wulfrun Hall
25th	London, Kilburn National
26th	Chester, Northgate Arena
28th	Leeds Metropolitan University
29th	Glasgow, Barrowlands
30th	Leicester De Montford University

May
1st	Portsmouth, Pyramid
3rd	Cardiff University

Summer
May
21st	USANew York Wetlands
24th	Manchester Nynex Arena (supporting Manic Street Preachers)

June
10th	BBC London (Later With Jools Holland TV show).
20th	Netherlands. Amsterdam Melkweg
21st	Germany. Hurricane Festival
24th	Lancaster, Cartmel College
29th	Glastonbury, Festival

July
2nd	Norway.	Quart Festival
5th	Denmark.	Midfyns Festival
6th	Holland.	Metropolis
8th	Italy.	Naples (supporting David Bowie)
11th	Belgium	Dour.
13th	Scotland	Balado, (Kinross T In The Park)
15th	Spain.	Madrid (supporting David Bowie)
16th	Spain.	Barcelona (supporting David Bowie)
17th	Spain.	San Sebastian

Seahorses USA & Canada Tour.
July
31st	USA. Providence,	

August
1st	USA.	Boston, Paradise Rock Club
2nd	USA.	Philedelphia, Theatre Of Living Arts
4th	USA.	Washington, Black Cat
5th	USA.	New York, Irving Plaza
7th	Canada.	Montreal, Foufounes
8th	Canada.	Toronto, Opera House
9th	USA.	Cleveland, Embassy
10th	USA.	Detroit, St Andrews
12th	USA.	Chicago, Metro
13th	USA.	Milwaukee, The Rave
14th	USA.	Minneapolis, Fine Line Music Cafe
15th	France.	St. Malo Festival
16th	Chelmsford, V97 Hylands Park	
17th	Leeds, V97 Temple Newsam	

Seahorses Tour resumed.
19th	USA.	Denver, Ogden Theatre
20th	USA.	Salt Lake City, DV8 Utah
22nd	USA.	Portland, La Luna
23rd	Canada.	Vancouver, Rage
24th	USA.	Seattle, Showbox
26th	USA.	San Francisco, Bimbo's
27th	USA.	Los Angeles, Palace
28th	USA.	Los Angeles, Viper Room
29th	USA.	San Diego, Cane's
30th	USA.	Las Vegas, Viva
31st	USA.	Phoenix, Cat Club

September
3rd	USA.	New York, CMJ Showcase (headlining)

October
1st	Southampton University
3rd	Sheffield University, Foundry
5th	Edinburgh, Assembley Rooms
6th	Lancaster, Sugarhouse
7th	Nottingham, Rock City
9th	Essex University
10th	Norwich, UEA
11th	Manchester, Academy
13th	Birmingham, Que Club
14th	London Astoria

DISCOGRAPHY

September 1995/Take It Easy Chicken/(Sci Fi Hi Fi Mansun 1 7")
November 1995/Skin Up Pin Up/Flourella/(Sci Fi Hi fi Beg 3)
March 1996/Egg Shaped Fred./(Parlophone CDR 6430)
June 1996/Take It Easy Chicken/Skin Up Pin Up /(CD 6437)
September 1996/Stripper Vicar/No One Knows Us //Stripper Vicar/The Edge/ The Duchess/(CDRS6447)
November 1996/Wide open Space/Klones/(Parlophone CDR 6454)
February 1997/She Makes My Nose Bleed/The Holy Blood And The Holy Grail/(Parlophone CD 6458)
/UKCD Part Two. She Makes My Nose Bleed/The /Holy Blood And The Holy Grail/Live Open Space/Drastic Surgeon
(Live) /(Parlophone CDRS 6458)
April 1997/Taxloss/Grey Lantern /Taxloss (The Lisa Marie/Experience remix)(Parlophone CDRS 6465)
October 1997/(CD1)/Closed For Business/K.1.Double/Everyone Must Win/The World's Still Open/(CD2)Closed For
Business/Dark Mavis/(Acoustic)/Stripper Vicar (Live)/Multimedia/Section featuring CD Rom of complete Taxloss
/video)

February 1997/Attack Of The Grey Lantern (Parlophone LC0299)
The Chad Who Loved Me/Mansun's Only Love /Song/Taxloss/You. Who Do You Hate/Wide /Open Space/Stripper
Vicar/Disgusting/She /Makes My Nose Bleed/Naked Twister/Egg /Shaped Fred/Dark Mavis.

(Mansun rarities abound. The most desirable currently being the Taxloss 12" promo including
remixes from John 00 Fleming, Slam, L-Mex and Guadi (12RDJ6465), an Interview Picture Disc
(CDUK 2. 6.97) and a 'tinned' version of Attack Of The Grey Lantern , Japan).

Chapter One	Mark Sutherland NME • Paul Moody NME • Mark Beaumont NME • Mike Pattenden Times Metro • Chester Chronicle
Chapter Two	Mark Beaumont NME • Chester Chronicle
Chapter Three	John Robinson NME • Paul Moody NME • Mark Beaumont NME
Chapter Four	Martin Aston Q Magazine • Simon Williams NME
Chapter Five	Mark Beaumont NME • Mike Pattenden Times Metro
Chapter Six	South China Morning Star • Mark Beaumont NME • Michael Mackey Liverpool Echo
Chapter Seven	Mark Beaumont NME

Picture credits

Front Cover   Hayley Madden/SIN

Chapter One   p3 Peter Anderson/SIN • p5 Robin/RETNA • p7 Peter Noble/SIN • p10-11 Ian T Tilton/SIN

Chapter Two   p13 David Buchan/REDFERNS • p16-17 Lili Wilde/ALL ACTION

Chapter Three   p23 Martyn Goodacre/SIN • p24 Melanie Cox/SIN • p26-27 Lili Wilde/ALL ACTION •
p28 Ed Sirrs/RETNA • p32-33 Hayley Madden/SIN

Chapter Four   p35 Justin Thomas/ALL ACTION • p36-37 Simon Meaker/ALL ACTION • p38-39 Steve Double/RETNA•
p42 Nigel M Adams/REDFERNS

Chapter Five   p49 Robin/RETNA • p50 Robin/RETNA • p52 Robin/RETNA • p55 Robin/RETNA •
p58-59 Tony Mott/SIN

Chapter Six   p61 R Chambury/ALPHA • p62-63 Simon Ritter/REDFERNS • p65 Nigel M Adams/REDFERNS •
p67 Ed Sirrs/RETNA • p68 Alan Glazier/ALL ACTION • p72 Dave Benett/ALPHA

Chapter Seven   p75 Ed Sirrs/RETNA • p78-79 Alan Glazier/ALL ACTION • p82-83 Nigel M Adams/REDFERNS •
p86-87 Steve Double/RETNA

The author and publishers have made every reasonable effort to contact all copyright holders. Any errors that may have occurred are inadvertent and anyone who
for any reason has not been contacted is invited to write to the publishers so that a full acknowledgement may be made in subsequent editions of this work.